Library of Congress Cataloging-in-Publication Data

Back, Christine.
   Bean and plant.

    (Stopwatch books)
    Includes index.
    Summary: Follows the development of a bean plant
from the emergence of the first tiny shoot to the
appearance of flowers and bean pods.
    1. Beans—Development—Juvenile literature.
2. Faba bean—Development—Juvenile literature.
[1. Beans—Development] I. Watts, Barrie, ill.
II. Title. III. Series.
QK495.L52B317 1986   583'.322   86-9634
ISBN 0-382-09300-3
ISBN 0-382-09286-4 (lib. bdg.)

First published by A & C Black (Publishers) Limited
35 Bedford Row, London WC1R 4JH

© 1984 A&C Black (Publishers) Limited

Published in the United States in 1986
by Silver Burdett Press,
Englewood Cliffs, New Jersey

Acknowledgements
The artwork is by B L Kearley Ltd.

Bean and plant

Christine Back
Photographs by Barrie Watts

Stopwatch books

Silver Burdett Press • Englewood Cliffs, New Jersey

This bean has been planted in the soil.

Have you ever had beans for dinner?
The beans that we eat are soft and green.

Look at the photograph. This bean is dry and brown.
It has been planted in the soil. The bean takes in
water from the damp earth. Soon a new plant will
start to grow from the bean.

This book tells you how the new bean plant grows.

A tiny root grows out of the bean.

On the outside of the bean there is a hard brown skin. This bean is split in half so that you can see inside it.

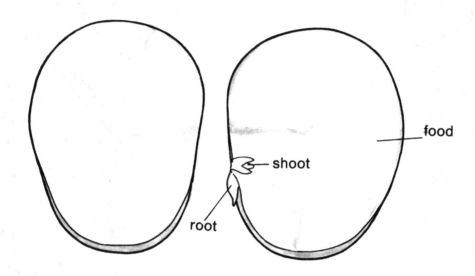

Can you see the tiny root and the tiny shoot inside the bean? The rest of the bean is a store of food. The root and the shoot will use this food when they begin to grow.

Look at the photograph. The root is beginning to grow. It has pushed through the hard skin of the bean.

The root gets longer. The shoot begins to grow.

Here is the root growing down into the soil.

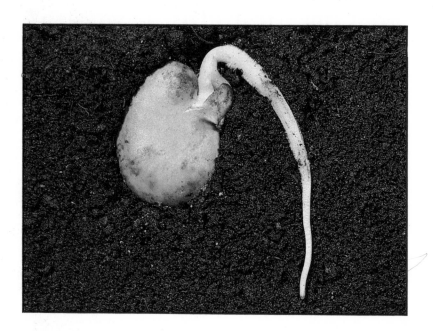

After fourteen days, a shoot grows out of the bean.
The shoot grows upward. Look at the big photograph.
Can you see the tiny yellow leaves on the end of
the shoot? The leaves curve downward so that they
are not broken as the shoot grows.

The root and the shoot need food to help them grow.
They are using up the food in the bean.

The shoot grows above the ground.

After eighteen days, the shoot pushes through the top
of the soil. Now the leaves are growing above the ground.

The leaves look like this.

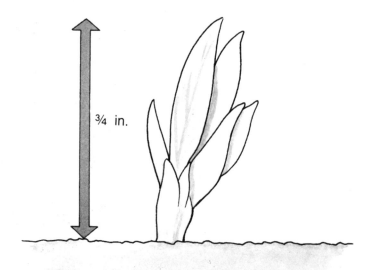

¾ in.

When the leaves are in the sunlight, they turn green.
Look at the photograph. You can see the leaves above
the ground and the roots under the ground.

The young plant grows more roots.

Now the plant has lots of little roots that grow from one thick root.

Here is part of the thick root.

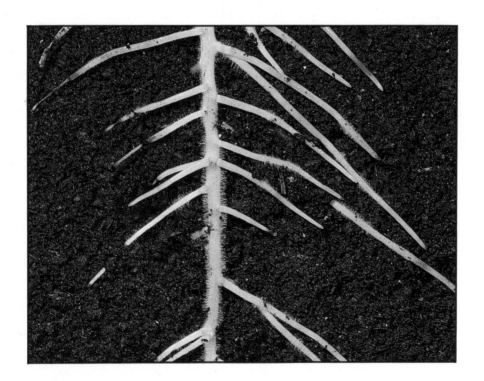

Can you see the tiny hairs on the root?
These hairs take in water from the soil.
The plant needs water to live and grow.

The plant needs food to help it grow.

The plant has used up all the food which was in the bean.
Soon the bean will shrivel up, like the one on this plant.

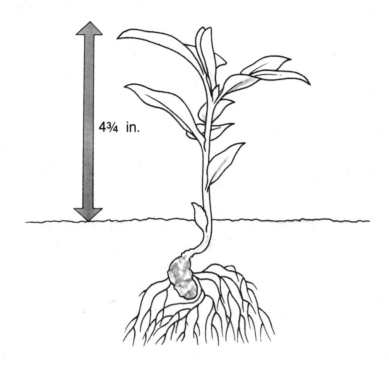

4¾ in.

Now the plant must make its own food. To do this,
the plant needs water, sunlight, and air.

The roots of the plant take in water, and the leaves
spread out to catch the sun. The plant gets air
through tiny holes in its leaves and stem.

The plant gets taller and grows more leaves.

After two months, the bean plant is more than twenty inches tall. Look at the photograph. The plant is so tall that it needs a stick to prop it up.

Slowly the plant gets bigger and taller. New stems grow from the main stem and more leaves grow.

This is what the plant looks like as it gets older.

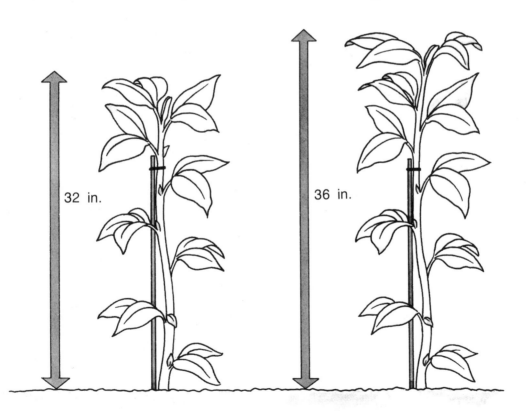

32 in.

36 in.

Flowers grow on the plant.

After three months the bean plant grows flowers, like this.

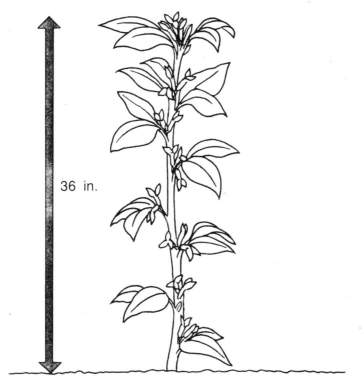

36 in.

Now look at the photograph. This is the top of a bean plant. Can you see the flowers?

Insects go into the flowers to find food. Inside the flowers, there is a yellow dust called pollen. Sometimes the insects get this pollen on their bodies.

The flowers die. Bean pods grow on the plant.

Look at this bee coming out of a flower.

Can you see the pollen on the bee's body? When the
bee goes into the next flower, some of this pollen
rubs off inside the flower. Then a tiny bean pod
may start to grow in this flower.

Soon the pod grows bigger and the flower dies.
Look at the photograph. Can you see the green pod
and the dead parts of the flower?

The bean pods grow bigger.

Here are some bean plants in a garden.

Can you see all the bean pods on the plants?
As the pods grow bigger, they hang down from the stems.
Look at the big photograph. This is how a bean pod
grows on the stem.

Inside the pod there are beans.

Look at the photograph. This bean pod has been cut
in half. Can you see the beans inside it?

Now it is time to take the beans out of the pod.
We can cook the beans and have them for dinner.
But we should leave some of the beans to dry.
Then we can plant them next year.

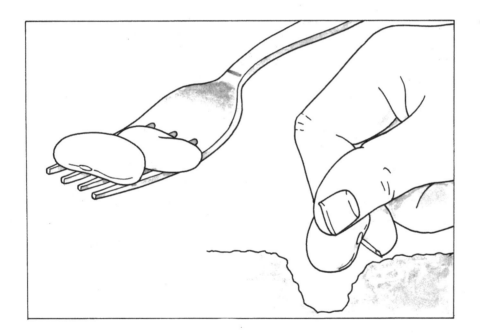

What do you think will happen when we plant the beans?

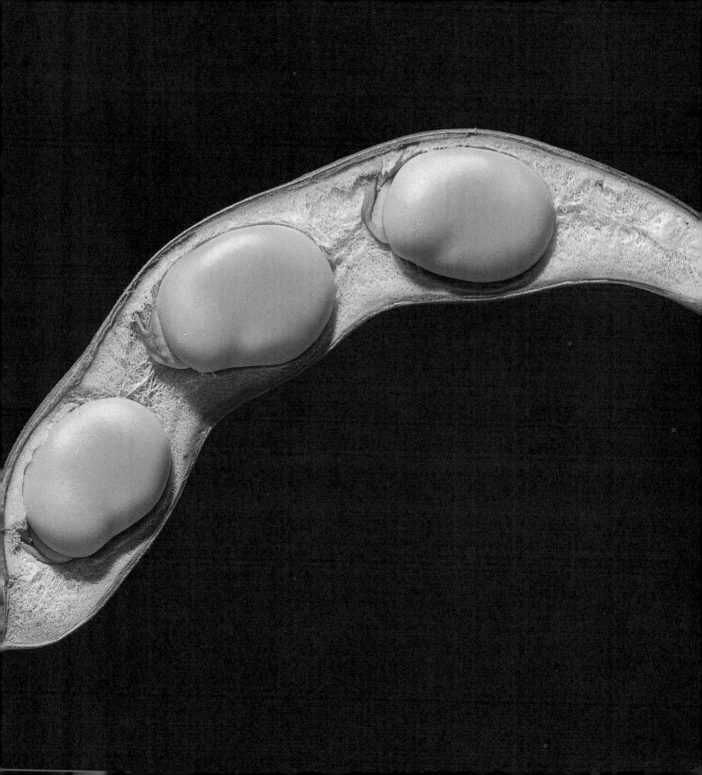

Do you remember how a bean plant grows?
See if you can tell the story in your own words.
You can use these pictures to help you.

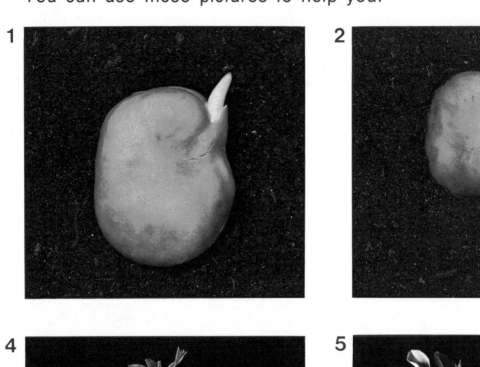

Index

This index will help you to find some of the important words in the book.

3

6

If you want to watch bean plants grow, try planting some in a pot or jar. But don't forget to water your plants.